Touch It!

Materials, matter and you

Written by **Adrienne Mason**
Illustrated by **Claudia Dávila**

Kids Can Press

Kids Can Press acknowledges the financial support of the Government of Ontario,
through the Ontario Media Development Corporation's Ontario Book Initiative; the
Ontario Arts Council; the Canada Council for the Arts; and the Government of Canada,
through the CBF, for our publishing activity.

Published in Canada by   Published in the U.S. by
Kids Can Press Ltd.   Kids Can Press Ltd.
25 Dockside Drive   2250 Military Road
Toronto, ON M5A 0B5   Tonawanda, NY 14150

www.kidscanpress.com

The artwork in this book was rendered in Photoshop.
The text is set in Century Gothic.

Edited by Valerie Wyatt and Christine McClymont
Designed by Julia Naimska
Science consultant: Jean Bullard

The hardcover edition of this book is smyth sewn casebound.
The paperback edition of this book is limp sewn with a drawn-on cover.
Manufactured in Tseung Kwan O, NT Hong Kong, China, in 6/2013 by
Paramount Printing Co. Ltd.

CM 05 0 9 8 7 6 5 4 3 2 1
CM PA 05 0 9 8 7 6 5 4 3 2

Library and Archives Canada Cataloguing in Publication

Mason, Adrienne
    Touch it! : materials, matter and you / written by Adrienne
Mason ; illustrated by Claudia Dávila.

(Primary physical science)
Includes index.
ISBN 1-55337-760-5 (bound). ISBN 1-55337-761-3 (pbk.)

1. Materials — Juvenile literature. 2. Matter — Properties — Juvenile
literature. I. Dávila, Claudia II. Title. III. Series.

TA403.2.M39 2005   j530   C2004-906569-6

Kids Can Press is a l'ORUS™ Entertainment company

Contents

A material world

Stone, metal, paper, plastic — these are different materials. Everything around you is made of some kind of material. A marble is made of glass, and this book is made of paper.

How many different materials can you see in the picture?

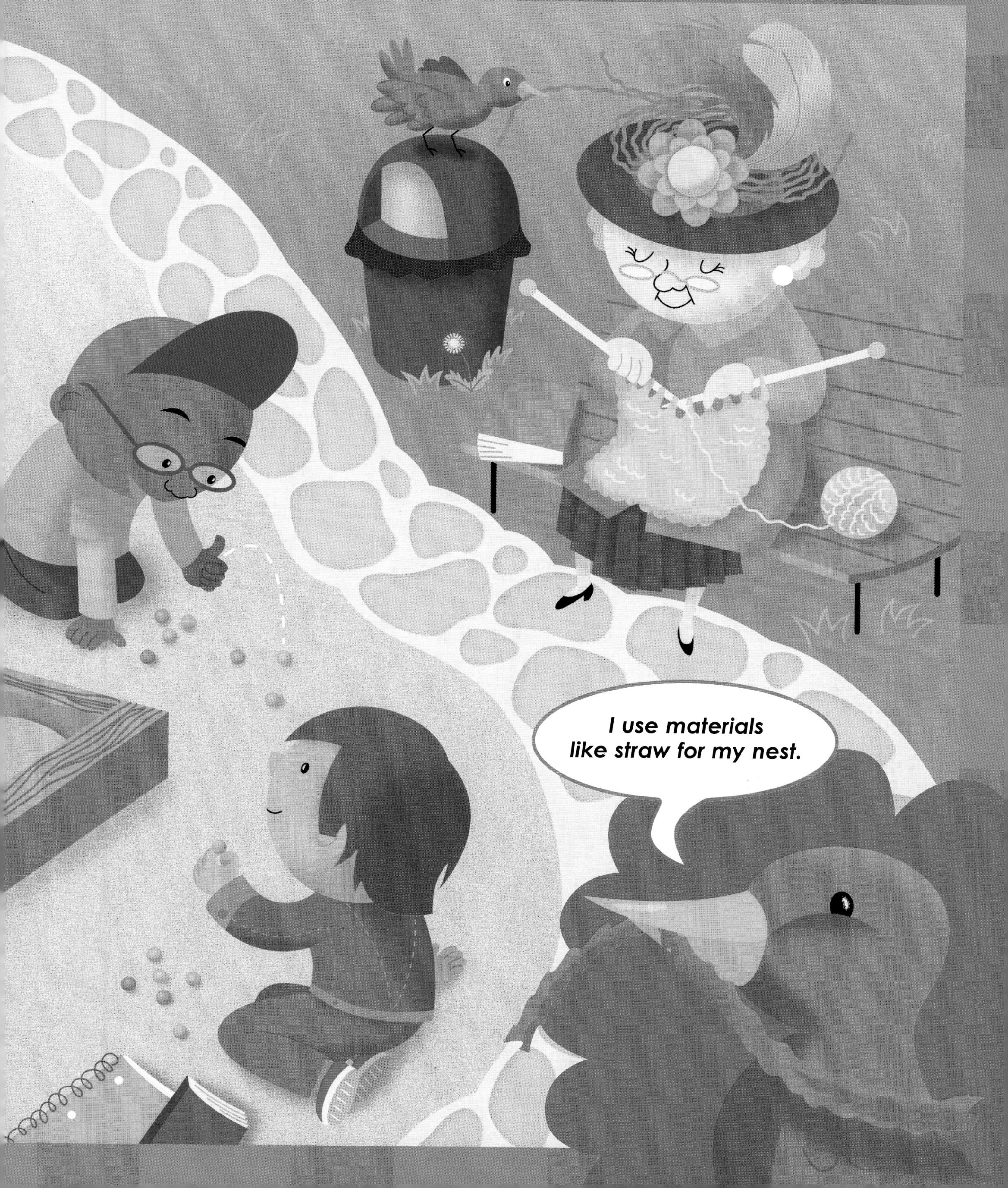
I use materials
like straw for my nest.

Material mosaic

Use different materials to make a mosaic picture.

You will need

- small objects made of different materials, such as stones, buttons, coins, beads, shells, pasta or seeds
- a muffin tin
- white glue
- a small piece of cardboard

What to do

1 Sort your objects into groups of the same material. You might have one group of stones, another of plastic objects and another of metal, for example. Use one muffin cup for each group.

2 Make a mosaic picture by gluing the objects to the cardboard.

What's happening?

Your picture is made of objects made from different materials. Some objects, such as a wood button, are made of one material. Other objects, such as pasta, are made of more than one material.

This tricycle is made of many different materials.

Describing materials

Different materials have different shapes, colors and sizes. A plum is round, purple and small. A banana is long, yellow and bigger than a plum. You can use your senses of sight, touch, smell, and even taste to describe materials.

How would you compare a strawberry and a pineapple?

Cherries are round, red, small and sweet. Yum!

Touchy materials

Different materials have different textures. Texture is the way something feels when you touch it. A rabbit's fur feels soft. A wood fence feels hard. Soft, hard, rough, smooth and prickly all describe textures.

What kinds of textures do the objects and creatures in this farmyard have?

How does it feel?

What are different textures used for? Try this guessing activity.

You will need
- a scarf
- several objects made of materials with different textures, such as a paper towel, bath towel, baking pan, piece of paper, sandpaper, hairbrush and ball of wool

What to do

1 Tie the scarf around a friend's eyes so she can't see.

2 Hand your friend different objects to touch. Have her describe the texture of each one.

3 Ask your friend to guess what each object might be used for.

What's happening?
Materials with different textures have different uses. A smooth piece of paper is good for writing on. Rough sandpaper helps to polish wood.

My fur is smooth and my tongue is rough.

Mass of materials

All materials, like these vegetables, have mass. Mass is the amount of stuff in an object. An object's mass can change when its size changes. As you grow, your mass will increase.

In the picture, which dog has more mass?

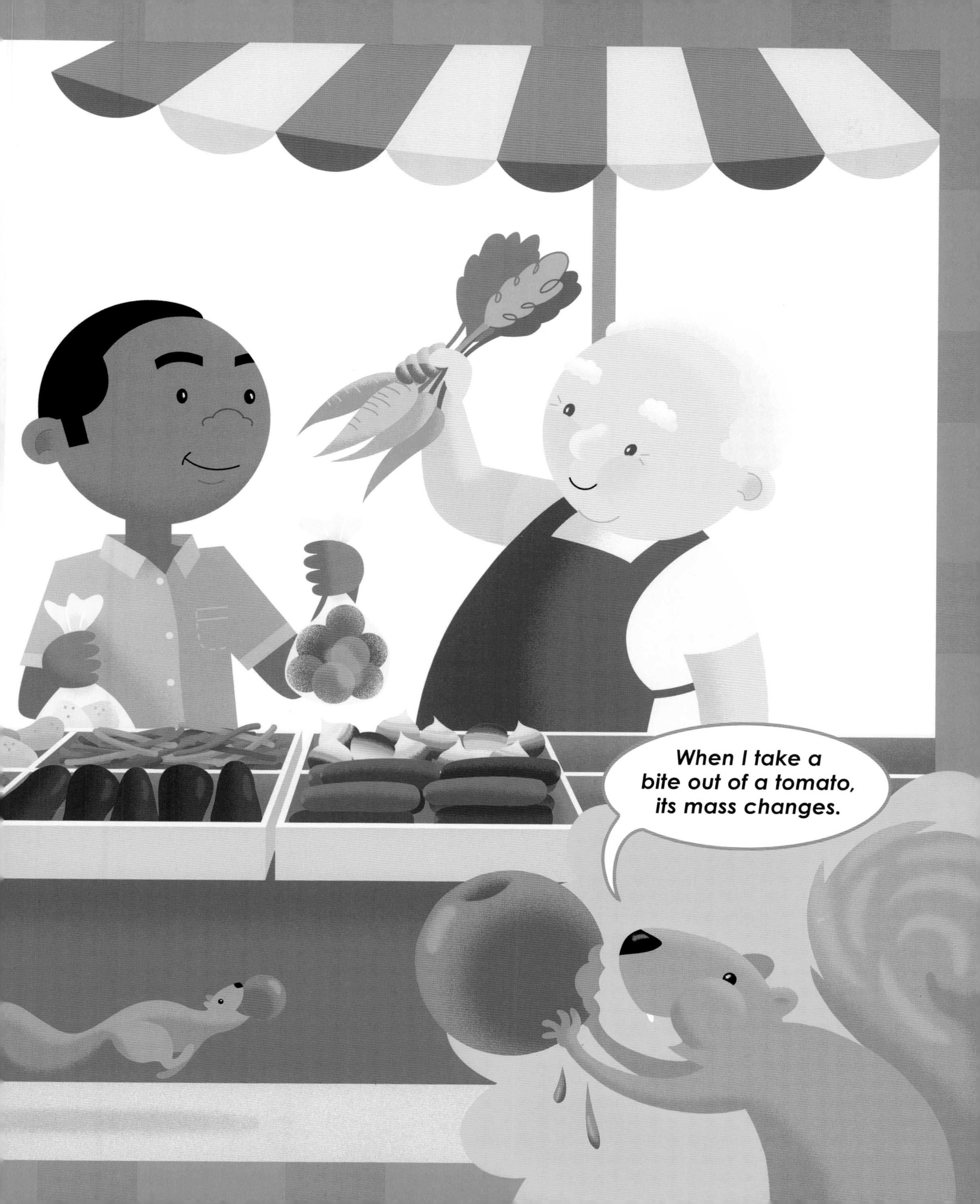
When I take a bite out of a tomato, its mass changes.

Comparing mass

Do objects of the same size, such as a coin and a button, have the same mass? Try this activity to find out.

You will need

- an eraser
- a ruler
- 2 paper drinking cups
- a coin
- a plastic button the same size as the coin

What to do

1 Place the eraser on its side. Balance the ruler on the eraser.

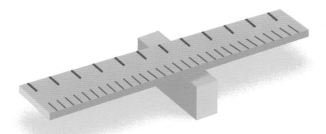

2 Put a paper cup on either end of the ruler. You have made a simple scale.

3 Place the coin in one cup and the button in the other. What happens?

4 Which has more mass, the metal coin or the plastic button? How do you know?

What's happening?

On your scale, the cup containing more mass will dip lower. Objects that are the same size but made of different materials often have a different mass.

This bowling ball has more mass than the soccer ball.

Floating materials

When a leaf falls onto a pond, it floats. But if you throw a stone, it sinks. Some materials float, while others sink.

The shape of an object can make a difference. A ball of clay will sink. But if you shape it into a boat, it will float.

Magnetic materials

You can use a magnet to attach a picture to your fridge, but not to a window or a table. Why not?

Some materials are magnetic. The kind of metal in this fridge door is magnetic, but glass and wood are not. Magnets attract magnetic materials. They pull toward one another.

Magnetic attraction

Which materials are magnetic? Find out with this activity.

You will need

- a magnet
- a number of small objects, such as a paper clip, key, marble, coin, eraser, nail, crayon, cork and stone

What to do

1 Without using the magnet, try sorting your objects into two groups — magnetic and not magnetic.

2 Now use the magnet to test all of the objects. Did you sort them into the correct groups? Which ones are magnetic?

What's happening?

Only objects made of metal materials are magnetic. Many types of metal are magnetic, but some metals are not. Objects made of other materials, such as plastic and glass, are not magnetic.

Using materials

Certain materials are used to make certain objects. Glass is a good material for windows. It is clear, so you can see through it. Metal, cloth and rubber are useful for other things.

Look at this picture. What are the objects made of? Why are those materials good for these objects?

The materials used in my helmet need to be strong and light.

Stretchy materials

Do some materials stretch more than others?

You will need
- one strip each of plastic wrap, newspaper, plastic grocery bag, paper towel and waxed paper, about 2 cm x 20 cm (1 in. x 8 in.)

What to do

1 Hold one end of the strip of plastic wrap firmly. Have your friend hold onto the other end.

2 Pull on the ends. What happens?

3 Try pulling on the other materials. Which material stretches most? Why do you think it needs to stretch?

What's happening?

Some materials are stretchier than others. Plastic wrap is stretchy so that it can be used to seal food tightly in containers. Newspaper, paper towels and waxed paper do not have to be as stretchy because they have different uses.

The material in my web is strong and stretchy — good for catching insects.

Materials around us

Objects are made of different materials.
Certain materials are better for certain uses.

Some materials float.

Some materials stretch.

Some
materials
are hard.

Some
materials
are soft.

For parents and teachers

The information and activities in this book are designed to teach children about materials, their properties and their uses. Here are some ways you can help them explore the concepts further.

A material world, pages 4–5
Ask children to look for places where the same type of material has different uses. For example, glass can be used in windows, in drinking glasses or in eyeglasses. Explain the difference between objects and materials. A cup is an object; it can be made of materials such as porcelain, glass, paper or plastic.

Material mosaic, pages 6–7
Have children look for objects that are made of one material (e.g., a drinking glass) and those made of several different materials (e.g., toys made with metal and plastic). They could sort the objects they collect for the activity in this way as well. Pasta, for example, is made of two materials — flour and water.

Describing materials, pages 8–9
Shape, color and size are properties of materials. Have children sort and describe objects using words for shape, color and size. Encourage them to use their senses of sight, touch and smell to describe materials, but make sure "taste" is used only for foods. Hearing can be used also: lightly tap a pencil against metal, glass, ceramic, wood and plastic objects and have children describe the sounds.

Touchy materials, pages 10–11
Texture is a property of materials. Ask children to find objects with many different textures. Encourage them to compare the textures of similar objects and discuss how texture relates to each object's use. For example, why do running shoes or hiking boots have rough soles, while dancing shoes have smooth soles?

How does it feel?, pages 12–13
Discuss how the texture of an object gives a clue as to how it might be used. For example, the rough texture of a paper towel suggests that it would be better for absorbing liquid than the smooth texture of a sheet of writing paper.

Mass of materials, pages 14–15
Mass is a property of materials. The mass of an object is how much matter it contains. An object's mass is always the same, regardless of where it is in the universe. In contrast, weight is a measure of the force of gravity acting upon an object. So weight varies according to where in the universe an object is. At this age, children don't need to know the difference between mass and weight, but be sure they use the correct term — mass — when comparing objects.

Comparing mass, pages 16–17

Have ready a variety of objects that are the same size but made of different materials. Ask children to compare their mass. They will discover that objects may be the same size, but if they are made of different materials their mass may vary.

Floating materials, pages 18–19

Buoyancy is a property of materials. Demonstrate how changing the shape of an object can sometimes change its buoyancy. Put a lump of clay in a bowl of water and watch it sink. Then shape it into a boat and watch it float. Children could test the buoyancy of similarly-sized objects made of different materials. For example, cut a piece of cardboard to the same size as a coin and try to float both objects.

Magnetic materials and Magnetic attraction, pages 20–23

Magnetism is a property of materials. Magnets attract objects made of the metals iron, nickel and cobalt. A magnet will pick up objects such as pins, nails and paper clips because they are made of steel, which contains iron. Children could use magnets to find magnetic and non-magnetic materials in the classroom or at home. Keep magnets away from computers and cards with magnetic stripes.

Using materials, pages 24–25

Have children sort objects into groups and see what materials are used for these objects. In a classroom, scissors, pencils, crayons, erasers, paper and other school supplies could be sorted. What kinds of materials are used in each type of object? Why are certain materials better for certain uses? For example, why are scissors made of metal and not wood?

Stretchy materials, pages 26–27

Flexibility is a property of materials. Some materials stretch farther before they tear or snap. Plastics are made of molecules that are strong and stretch quite a bit before they break. Papers are made of fibers that are not as strong. Have children describe the uses of objects that are made of stretchy materials such as plastic wrap, rubber, elastic and stretchy fabrics.

Materials around us, pages 28–29

Buoyancy, stretchiness and hardness are properties of materials. Size, color, shape, texture, transparency, mass and magnetic attraction are also properties of materials. Challenge children to choose one object and describe at least three different properties of the materials used in that object. Encourage them to use as many of their senses as they can.

Words to know

magnetic: can be attracted by a magnet

material: what an object is made from

mass: the amount of stuff in an object

texture: how something feels to the touch

Index